L U S I O N S

LUSIONS
James Ragan

Grove Press
New York

Grateful acknowledgment is made to the following publications, in which these poems originally appeared: *Hampden-Sydney Review,* "On Mowing a Lawn"; *New Letters,* "The Dogs of China," "August 19, 1991," "The Holy Ghost as Eighth Grader"; *Nimrod,* "The Birth of God (from an Early Photograph)," "Dreaming a Flood of Conscience"; *The Review,* "The Vineyards at Bar Sur Aube"; *Trafika,* "The Mayor Boils a Speck of Dust," "Anniversary of a Roman Arch"; *Southern California Anthology,* "The Refugees of Tuzla," "Two Kinds of Darkness"; *Mississippi Valley Review,* "The Willow Father"; *Windsor Review,* "An Immigrant Playing Violin in the Neighbor Wood."

Published simultaneously in Canada
Printed in the United States of America

FIRST EDITION

Library of Congress Cataloging-in-Publication Data
Ragan, James, 1944–
    Lusions / James Ragan.—1st ed.
      p.   cm.
    ISBN 0-8021-1603-5
    I. Title.
    PS3568.A39L87   1997
    811'.54—dc20   96-35090

Design by Laura Hammond Hough

Grove Press
841 Broadway
New York, NY 10003

10 9 8 7 6 5 4 3 2 1

FOR MY BROTHERS AND SISTERS:

John, Andy, Paul, Mary,
Al, Theresa, Anka, Joseph,
Michael, Helen, George, and Tom

FOR ALLOWING TRUTH
TO DISAGREE
WITH HISTORY'S AGREED LIES.

If you ask what it is I am here to

do in this world, I will tell you.

I am an artist. I am here to live out loud.

Émile Zola

L U S I O N S

Lusions

In the laugh belly of too little thought,
a lusion is eating up the mind
for nothing. It needs no compensation
for the distance it will travel or the time
it takes to eat the hum of reason
out of tongues. It is only the brief

nuisance of its love for laughter
that keeps the mind whole.
In the laugh belly of our prehistoric skulls,
lusions like tumors in the brain
grow secret terrors into what is taught.
Each day our hunger turns to silence,
we lose another thought.

I / ALLUSION
Prehistory

The Birth of God (*from an Early Photograph*)
IN MEMORIUM, THEODORE VON KARMAN

At first silence, a gas or two, a wind unchallenged
as if some breath were conspiring to leap a word
across oblivion. It was to be a universe
of light and sound and calm, ethereal,
a way to mirror a god's mirage through vanity,
but still this wind,

                         its whisper like a protest
growing syllables, echoes that would not wane.
It was to be a simple creation. An exercise at most
of mischief, to play at quarks like building blocks,
replenished and diminished, and by its cycle
a god might gain dominion. We would call it nature.
And still this wind,

                         a pest, perplexing, by some quirk
of fate escaped the boundaries of imagination.
And worse, it grew aloof, a mind of its own
filled with thoughts of relative notions.
What next, a march, a sit-in, a declaration of rights?
By god, there could be no negotiation.
Until the wind

had found the future willing,
it named itself HAVOC, and in its wake
propelled the span of the "Galloping Gertie,"
winding her last ride down the ocean narrows.
Above the gimballed truss the gods of intellect convened
as if to find what workings of its mind they failed
to civilize or redeem,

what renegade, what sorcery
of force prepared the eddies of its face,
or since one could not know its face,
that cylindrical, funneled tunnel of eyes
which glowered space like oscillating plumes?
What velocity! What shear flow. What HAVOC wombed,
the gods would overthrow.

Until in boundless words
against the gabled Atheneum like some histrion
Bogarting the Mach abyss of sound, a voice, sudden
as a quantum leap, spoke the syllable of repair,
"wind." "I represent only the wind." And HAVOC
swooned a kiss, and in a mortal gust of whim, married
all of gravity to space.

Thus had God created human nature,
a necessary fiction, like turbulence out of ruins
so passionate even the good lord could not presume.
To the gods of intellect, nothing contained remained
at absolute rest. To man, nothing soared so fickle
as wind and out of reach he wouldn't chase it
to the moon.

The Pebble Culture

When in Greenland the ice had slid
its one broad shelf across the plains,
pushing past the rise of stone and lava,
and arctic ferns had split their roots
between the tarn and tundra
not knowing which, the thorn or reedbuck,
they had fed or fathered, one stone struck
steep against the other, chips flaking
off the white spurs of fire,
and a girl in her Choukoutien cave
of burnt bones and antlers, carved
her bowl into a hollow, the rough shape
incised into the curvature of a breast,
now mothering, now flowered, and the boy,
who saved the razor edge of the glacier flake
for his own picking, grazed the Abbevillian ax
against the wall, a shower of pebbles
forming in their meteoric light
frenzied points of departure, spoons into knives,
flint into spears, violence into culture.

The Reindeer Age

When sculpting down the bison skull
with a finer bone, sheer as glass,
he saw his hand at once an instrument
of will, no longer formed to father stone,
the rhythm in the stroke an even pull,
and over it the wind, wooden in its skin,
scraped the lash and water dry,
the caves of eyes still soaking
brows where once the sight had been.

Always at the point where shape was born,
where out of stillness, calm had tamed
the bison's palled belligerence,
and where on walls the reindeers danced
in briers as in flames, there remained
a thinking, prejudiced and small,
that skilled in images of chase, bones
would hack the skull's Solutrean intelligence;

that where the caribou slept in wait
along the mindscape's blunt horizon,
a hunter, knowing only the hand as stone,
would sling his bolas, wind to forehead, not as craft
or as logic one mind gives the other,
but as power striking down the sprawl of antlers,
muscling up the dark veins of the skull.

The Pit Fall

Hear the grunting thighs descend,
how approaching water in a field,
the wildebeest stumbles,
something like a boulder
that puddles into muscle. Something balled
and steep as waves inciting gravity.
He does not grow to gallop well
and prone to stagger, will not see
the pit slap up its tongueless cave
to lick the sleeve of heaven.

He will gnaw with hooves the brittle walls
to meet the club that bleeds in darkness.
When, in hands that hoist him
up and onto land, his horns are twisted
once to snap the stem, twice to graze the fire,
only tendons know what strength
the brain would dare imagine,
how the motor in us all has rived
through veins to breach a primal force,
how at death the body finds no use at all
for memory and where the mind has been.
Nor does it matter.

Birthing a Daughter into the Holocene Epoch

On walls she watches her limbs unfolding,
creased beneath the heart's cage;
a sleek gazelle obsessed
with simple leaps of daring,

she is forever hurdling
the fields of her own body.

Arching sky-high
as if to race a lion to some African star,
she pursues now the shy
stalled flight of a fleeing fawn.

This is how she lies each night,
foraging fists along the bed or ceiling

like some competition where a line is drawn.
Gradually the moon appears. She resumes
until the deer she corners in her arm
and cradles, smothers in her grip.

Now she lies all day unfolding
back her long sleep arm.

Embracing once the finger's lobe,
now the palm's indenture, she inhales,
creasing her eye's final fold closed,
certain like the lion she grows eternal.

13

The Eskimo's Twelve Expressions of White

FOR MIROSLAV HOLUB

I
Iced on the bone
bridge of the eye,
a tear glances at a fire.

II
An ibex sleeping
on the steppes
of the great Siberian snow
becomes the moon's horizon.

III
Fog crawls in
at the lip of a lake.
An Aleutian dog has laid down
his steaming breath
to praise a mountain.

IV
In the eye's reflection
stalactite, seeding water,
drips down the hanging scarf
of a cave, now warming.

V
The twenty spears
of a reindeer's horn
bleed before the fish man
whittles bones to eyelets.

VI
The harpoon towing
the whale's white fin
across the Bering Strait
stiffens to track the marmot.

VII
To outrun the elk,
a snow hare lunges deep
into the throat of a glacier.

VIII
A snowbank drifts in the
wind.
The bear's tracks limp
back to the lost logs of fire.

IX
The starved harp seal,
moled to higher ground,
laps at the light of the Aurora.

X
Water soaks the fur of the stoat.
His weasel coat browns
to ermine in winter.

XI
Within the spined avalanche of hair,
a woolly mammoth sleeps,
frozen in the mountain's skull.

XII
The fire
at the bone bridge of the eye
glances at a tear, now warming.

II / DELUSION
The Age of Darkness

Two Kinds of Darkness

I

THE ANNUNCIATION
When calling sleep down each night
as law required, her mother whispered, boily girl,
in dark there is a light no one sees
as through the underskin of stone the worm turns to
from its tunneled earth side, it somehow weens
the monster eye of the forager crow.
In your eyes too, a transparency
rives beneath the lids.
At twelve years old, blind
in the granite alcove fashioned for a bed,
she saw the dark's reflection of dark
riffling along the eyescape's wall
like shimmering webs. And she studied
the imagined eye outside eyeing her nakedness.
Beyond the latticed roof in boily darkness,
she saw light and in its eyes the white
sinewy sails of long grackles' wings.

2

CONCEPTION

This was her all-child's imagination.
On rain-days in bed beneath the angel's creak of dark,
the boily girl would see the monster shrike
attack her eyes' transparent panes
with timbrel feet and pedaling claws.
Above the flapping wings and rafter's thunder,
she could see her body's soul in flight depart.
                    Sometimes too, in lovemaking,
as she passed her years in passion as law required,
she still heard thunder's splash of lightning
repeat the rearranging of the summer sky.
And she'd hear a voice call down sleep, boily
like whispers spilled in space, ephemeral, distant.
She studied the imagined light between each body toss,
and in her eyes, the dark
no one saw, the crow's sky dominion,
wings still fluttering to leave.

The Invention of Horsebrass

It was forbidden to graze with eyes
along the far pasture of the sky,
to see what stars had seen
before the universe had burned to rocks,
bewitched by songs of the cockatrice
and naked in the rain of light.

Long before the sun and crescent
led each horse and ox to harrow earth,
long before their minds had formed to muscle,
and worse their aspirations bowed to harness
the battle will of generations,
an evil eye, transfixed in clouds

above the flowered oaks of Dover
like some winged and taloned harpy,
spoke the tongues of serpents,
hissing at the hooves to stop, lie down,
and die awhile. It was forbidden for farmers
to daydream into beauty the glide of crows

whose haunting flutters lulled the ears of lambs.
In such fear where stock would die of darkness
and ravens swooned in daylight as in night,
brass, the holy amulet, mystic in its reflection,
redeemed the powers of the nether light,
the beast in every man.

The Burghers of Calais, 1347

What gilded chaplet, halting the King's tumbrel,
would each of the six in chains inherit
when by offering their souls, the siege, sustained
beyond a year, now paused to barter heads?

Surely, they were politic at first, assuming
trades were made for little more than grievance,
a passage through to Norman lands, perhaps,
a crown or chest from the Pope's exchequer.

But to save Calais, a town dismembered, wormed
by plague like rations bled from horses,
to what good would silks and pewter matter,
if by nature Edward saw the royal chance to rule

each hostage with his greed to conquer heaven.
What, in hand, a wingless gannet, rose, or shroud
first persuaded Philippa's intercession,
giving pity to the world so great a monument

that in the phalanx Rodin had carved, he bronzed
her heart and laid it at the center, each peel of metal,
pulsing as eternal and pure a courage as any
the burghers might inspire in the parliament of men?

The Margin of Error

As if to bait the Inquisitor
like some bear he'd nipped and lanced,
Galileo had no sooner paired meridians
as arcs of destinations
or halves of circles to a whole,
than giving up the globe to chance,
he qualified the error, recanting
how it had a way of falling
three points more or less
in margins far from the stabilizing force.
Give us each exacting polls, he said,
like the Greenwich clock or metronome
or the Angelus whose noonday toll
leaves no longitude of distance
between blind faith and the Pope.
Give us latitude to hope.
Show us truth or the precision of the sudden
as with the shattering of glass
all heads will turn at once
to the unifying moment beyond.
And the Bishop grew defiant.
Show us a miracle in a spinning earth, he roared,
how it moves through space
with no apparent aim or reason,
you who walk on grass
because you believe that stones lament.

Epitaph to the Plumber of Westminster Abbey

Here lies in the nave of the South Cloister,
among such poets who squeeze into each corner space
their wanton worms of sonnets,
                    the body of Philip Clark,
Plumber to this Collegiate Church, who in haste
Dep. ted life this 21 st of Sep er 1607
in the 43 rd Year of his Age,
                    who from his crusted hypocaust
conducts the business of the day
advising bishoprics that they are safe
in their remains.
                    Lord of pipes,
he fascinates the sky and higher peers of royalty
whose bones beneath his sewage ducts
rust red in winter as in May.
                    He is accused
of no thing sinful, his life as admirable
as sons. To his wife, the King of Briton's
snores are greater than any wrong
                    he might have done.
But having so dis pleased the chancellery
in whose usury Luther grieved at Worms,
he failed to turn off
                    the water valve
to the Archbishop's private seat,
and pumping tons of drainage, flooded
the heads of religion
                    and half the minds of state.

Myth and the Higher Orders of Abstraction

When once we are the myths we gather in,
who guides our thoughts to wicked wanderings,
some cold as a woodsman's ax, others
under touch, raw hot and breathing
syllables into lust? What failed delusion,

what salacious falling out of song
along the curled maps of tongues
follows wind into the wood hollows
of a barren forest? What pure note is love
of one thing for another, when sound
like an echoing bark inhabits silence?

The artist must always be forgiven.
He wants to believe in words that cannot lie,
in planets shooting by and dying as an art.
He would conceive of man a perfect nature
were it not for his grifter's heart

and tarred smoke wreathing out of lungs
black as grillage on a mantled cloth.
He is the son of his stars, creating
infinitely in every word
a universe of passion. Myth he saves
for the higher orders of abstraction.

III / ILLUSION
Enlightenment

Perizoma: On Striking Michelangelo's
Signature from the Pietà

As if a burr were pricking at the base of the brain,
a prompting so minute it fogs the ordinary
scan of roentgens viewing the mind's sfumato,
he felled the sixteenth blow. It is not known how
the hammer armed its way into the raincoat's sleeve,
if on the shaft the imprimatur was Italian,

or if an ironsmith whored his dye along a foreign metal.
What is known is how he strode the dark rotunda,
stoicly, unaware a mass had ended or that absence unforgiven
taints the sainted hall. He might have noticed,
had he searched Bernini's colonnade, a thurible
installed among the Pentecostal gyres,

how one mote of incense fans imagination,
that he might, himself, have been a sculptor
were he not Hungarian and lost in the economics of serving
sloth's collective purpose for the will of all.
Now here, perhaps, lies the motive, a rite of passage
like some grand design where fate belies the act. Anyhow,

while before the silky vein of marble, he raced
to pound the virgin skin, the inspiration, dulled perhaps,
from touching for the kingdom's evil, awakened in his head
to strike at all the senses, the nose, the lips, and last
the eyes' rude gift of resignation. Were it all as simple
as a quickening of passion, he'd wait, but no,

with each mounting flight of air his pounding stern resolve
now stiffened, he carved from the mantle's wimple
each letter like a body from a soul he'd willingly discard.
And by his signature dared the virgin stare to pity
art's imperfect balance; what unity of space so long assembled
the mind prepares to order, the heart resolves to break apart.

The Buttered Toast Mystery

Newton must have known
that toast falling off
the breakfast table
lands butter side down
because the universe
is planned
not as the perverse
toss of a mystic
chancing out his physics,
but of laws
born out of the pure
needs of annoyance,
that in order to descend
it is the mind's way
to lick at gravity
until the air is thinned,
until the apple's nose
resists
the testy ride of wind,
until the knee
to miss a stair
slips and stumbles
or a foot to sweep
below the rising bed
stubs its knuckle.

The aggravation
is clearly one of duty
to drive a mind to madness,
lubricious spasms,
and everywhere and in all descent
the toast's fall to earth
as in birth
remains unfair,
and always to its creator
seditious, inconvenient,
a pain in the derriere.

The Vineyards at Bar Sur Aube

In Urville it must have felt peculiar
to bevel earth so hard the axle stalled,
while both the vintner in his minting smock
and mayor at the gendarme's arm,
scratching at their skulls,
found instead of wining grass
a wall beneath the tractor's diggings
down where seeding's always best for stalks.

To find a Roman bath at all
in Urville is the talk of excavation,
that anyone should plant in drills
beyond the petty cache of grapes
a tress of bracelets, gold and bronze,
and of an empire's worth the Dauphin
might have blushed to see how history repeats
the excesses of his reign.

How exotic still the mosaic of a dolphin
and an ankle jewel which, on chance,
a swimmer bound with lacings on the Tiber,
lost unwinding on the Aube,
and loosed a myth untaught to generations,
that in the ivory of Lespugne, beauty flowed
from Gallic fonts to art's imagination;
the birth of Venus, unlimbed, unrobed.

Delacroix and the Organ at St. Sulpice

Hear the tumult beneath the painted glass
each now whistles, note to note,
sweet oboes to the ear, the song emerging once
as tin drops during rain, now as sunlight
sweeping dust along the nave.
How the walls, tune gray with sulfur, brighten
to the piping's tones. Hear the wind roam

the columns' daily grill, what calms
the air, what being still, grinds each hue
of green into a verse Verlaine had choired
out of dulcet blues into the spandrels?
Hear the brush now pitch in rhythm
against each vault and gyre
as if to jolt creation out of indecision.

Hear the splashing sun he brushes
swill each spoke of red into a wheel of light.
Music is a random rime of breath,
a storm of silence, violently composed.
Watch the star in flight, how it wanders
boldly into an eagle's darkest eye.
Hear each stroke burst permanently into fire.

Madame Rimsky-Korsakov: Peinture
at the Musée d'Orsay

a.
Her hand at the left breast clutching
larks of brown curls, Winterhalter
must have mourned to send it there,
his own, a brush in paint
regretting loss as too familiar.

He would rather part the fingers, each lithe stroke
a stranger teasing hair, unsexed, just so.
If only he could creep behind the canvas,
not to memorize which brown the eyes,

which green, which light magenta
most improves an unapproving face,
but to brood; could he undo the blue
ribbon where the heart lives? Or breathe
soft hues against the white lace?

He would stall the flow of resignation
each brow permits to spill into her eyes.
Where the bodice heaves beneath in rhythms
long and quiet, breath would part the space.

b.
Watch how jealousy's soft green feather
swells her husband's brow,
one eye traveling notes along the scale,
the other down her hair
to where the hand creates a rose.

If only he could undo the eyes' imagined veil,
languid where the soul dies
or mirror her thoughts
in the rush of a rising scherzo,

he would bare her breasts
to each eye's passing,
hurried once as tourists do,
now returned with voyeur passion.
If only he could father lust as inspiration.

To what picture at the exhibition should he turn?
When they creep behind the camera lens,
is it out of shame for having framed his wife,
undressed, a lover in their found imaginations?

Anniversary of a Roman Arch

An aroma of bilberry swills the river
across the boulevard. In a cafe
beneath a canvas skirting out its visor
or is it a linden, near absolute, now votive
in its blinding, you first sit and regret
to leave the city. You wait where the aroma
smokes conspicuously off the water.
On the boulevard, across from a Roman
arch at the Palais du Louvre,
you smell the swill of bilberries
filling space like myrrh in a pyramid,
filling the space of years
until it passes for a prophesy. It doesn't
repeat ever. The boulevard crosses all
that is your future. The only way
to come to death is backwards,
through the senses, remembering
the city, its aroma, memorizing the Gioconda,
how like the drift of leaves through a Roman arch
her smile could nearly stop the seasons.

IV / COLLUSION
In the Age of Atoms

Poem to the Photograph of a Found Daughter

TO DEBORA

Neither of you knew
that behind you on the white
hills in the photograph I took
the day after snow,

a fire was building on a cloud,
and the figure of a child, young Helen,
lost when the spring rains broke
and lured her brothers to German skies,

came forward on her sled, play-tired.
I remember her miles down the road
of Goldstrohm Lane before the cows were shed
and chickens loped, headless, along

father's hatchet rail. She'd twist
her glider rope, fist-tight, and with a running
start, angling down to speed,
fire that Rocket sled to earth

then breathe, feverishly, all the ride down
to the bottom of its glide. All my life
through six years old and cliffs of snow,
I've tunneled to retrieve her broken breath.

The August day she slept through
breakfast, play, and noon,
I promised her in bed, white and wreathed,
I'd bring the winter back. I promised her

a passage dog to spring. Photographs
I have learned to trust for their accuracy
and sisters for their running speed
and memory only for the truth

it hides in what we never see—Hiroshima.
Nothing is salvageable, found daughter,
angling home, clinging, fist-tight, and play-tired
to one more winter on your Rocket sled.

Antiques

After war the antique dealer swore
he saw the father on the knee of the field
mumbling obscenities to a son
he could not find in his memory's drift.

Damn it, damn you, damn this whip,
you antic hair on the napalm bough,
ant's umbilical to a zebra's hide,
fetish to an eyebrow's lash.

The dealer said he found the father lost,
an upright stalk of spile and ice
melting where the sow's feet
pick and shovel at the outdoor hut.
The horse could know no better
than to lick his sight off with the dung.

Damn you, whip, damn it, damn you, Cong,
echo's talker to the day behind,
tar remains of a Mekong skull,
plague and hobbler of a horse's ass.

The dealer swears he'd sell the child
a whip to own the father. A child's no horse,
the whip's not grass. The dealer says
it don't much matter. After war
the people lost ain't antiques you save
to pay for grain or fodder. They don't grow
expensive as they grow older.

The Dogs of China

Near the stubborn space of curbs
along the dining *hutongs,* wraiths
of bikesters rally down
the taxi trails on Fuxingmenwai.
At Tien An Men Square a dog on sight
invites the culinary art of dissection.
You will not see one near restaurants.

The Deng-Li camel, photo posing
at the Great Wall, alone, perhaps,
in his dramatic act of standing
still, shows a cunning
and a photogenic will to survive.
No one knows how or where each day
like the Sherpas in the Tibetan wood
he ascends the precipice of stone
without a rail to prevent his falling.

Even the Peking duck, exiled
in the wind drift of flight's protection,
quails beneath the butcher's ax
along the willow downs of Ritan Pond.
Nowhere is he safe from harbors.
Nowhere is the reach of wind
so swift he could seine
beyond man's touch and reason
in the wider, wilder moats of change.

August 19, 1991

I

THE COUP

All the sky needs mending.
The sun wings out like a white crow
from the skewered palm of the yard.
The oak has buried the birch,
and wind the hurricane awakes
uproots the Wainscott spinneys.

We have come a distance to be warned.
Fallen, the Russian mapmaker's hedge,
and scions from the roof's old tar
leave all boundaries bobbed and mourned.

My daughter, bold as a startled quail,
pokes about the parlor stalls
for books to shore and corner.
What progress does it matter
to the lurch of slugs along a window spur
that steps are momentary? She has crawled

beneath our stares to see the past beginning.
On the porch among the maps of wind's assemblage,
she reads a palimpsest of nature's poems
in fossils of the sky's remains.

She is starved for meaning
from words long fashioned. Who can rob
her generation of this wild wind's pleasure,
the once still wand of a lark's
broad throat, now a flutter
in the sudden choke of rain?

II

THE WIND

For years wind has been forcing out
a language from its breath.
Now the carpet walks itself to wood,
and candles have no space to light
but indirection. Outside, near the wall
of pear and apple ruins, starlings

build their greenhouse, tentacled as lungs,
and store the sun in spikes of brittle glass.
All night the fog rolls up in darkness.
Pines impale their needles underground.

In bed my daughter hears that thunder
on the Bay of Foros is a god of barrows
wheeling souls across a cobbled cloud.
Down the looms of runnels stars are falling.
Lightning clears the crusty ruck of sky.
I see my daughter light two candles

to our god's passing. With each wick's
burst of sun she whispers all to hush,
believing lies like ancient propagandas
warm the draft of passion in our thighs.

She still hopes along Crimean shores
to hear the lark's deep lung murmur
breathe into the rain and fly.
She still believes that conscience, uprooted,
like a timid beast at the swale of wind
will not fall silent.

Dreaming a Flood of Conscience

On the stone shallows of our basement floor,
ravaged where the whisper god of grass immortal
sleeps beneath snow and the bald
skull of the sky lies knee-high in the river,

a blade of ice pries the granite blocks,
stakes its nail to the dog's heart, bleeding.
My father at the noonday siren swears to pound down
all the children. In suspender straps

hung from the ceiling, we watch
all things driven by the snow stones
rive through the floor. Where it splinters,
heartless, a pair of tire irons

sinks first, and a willow shags bloodroot
like an uncle's box bumped about
down a grave lift. A hammer's claw
tunes our piano like a passing hedgerow.

All night the Saudi sand soldiers
burst through the Magnavox, birth-wet
and cracking, the electric lights of their eyes
blurring the sky like flares. And soon

a tube of bargain fur, flat-nosed
like a mole burrowed at the pane of a windowsill,
barges down the open road. The wind
plays bagpipes on its wattled snout.

My daughter cheers its quick escape
between two hounds as if to say life
goes on beyond mere death and the river.
Nothing, nothing we could save, we own.

Not the Saudi soil, not even the yard's stick snails
thawed down to their piano bones.
The same river after crest we bury
for our children, underground.

On Mowing a Lawn

1
Circling the backyard little by little,
a starling parts the feathers of a wing
and learns with space a falling,
how the bowl of the beak
leaves its sweet breath on the grass
and in our hearts the memory of sky lost.

At our memory's table, civilized, gluttonous,
and full of gain, we learn our minds
as in the last line of a riddle
or a poem juiced out of the happenstance of talk
we owe to our genius, come back for a spoon.

Genius eats with its fingers, politely,
and moves the ruins of a culture
across the whole space of a plate
until it is fed perfectly.

2
I mow a lawn and find in the yard
neighborings of minor gods, spreaths
of all-loving creatures, surviving on our loss.
Reason, sonar to the brain, divides

the half-sheened wings of gypsy moths,
the deep mound cave the mole rat
finds omnisciently in dark.
Now the mantis, self-adoring spawn of grass,
prays tall for all shears to stall.

I am genius around these parts.
I weed wings from the high rill's skull.
Until the mowed bone of something brittle
rattles still as dice. Until
my dog bares the shank of his teeth
at the slightest trespass or assault.

In his jowls the starling I have claimed
to love has been spleened perfectly.
By his bark he has lost faith in my ability
to transcend the limits of my nature.
It takes heart, not genius, to mow a lawn.

V / EXCLUSION
Braving the New World

The Refugees of Tuzla

Pray for the others born.
Their legs have known the absence
of air they are not walking today
in love with earth. Pray for their souls.
They have stepped down to everything
blown and dusting the ground.
Pray that their knees
like bones of chickens, chalked and beetled,
will not bend in adoration
to crows stippling the sky's talk wire.
Teach them to see how falsely
their toes are steeples to the eye
studying the language of darkness,
how in their longest stride
they might have shared
the pull and tug of a raven's run
in and out of the coop's locked sky.
They might have saved a step or two
from the womb's kick journey. Pray
that when they awake they will want to be
this sound and that, frog-low, finch-high.
Even as they die let them fall
through their deepest sleep
into the tall stretch of adolescence,
cock-walking the neighborhood, others
born in their first long pants.

For Three Twelve-Year-Old Homeboys

who have grown
too old for the diapered tribe
of cynics, spread-eagled
on the floor of the genius nursery,
who brave the mimed war
that street gang inhabitants now perform,
there is no seeing
everything as one and ordered.

The oldest, bandanna
toweled around his globed skin head,
signals to the slumlord
he is about to bloodlet out of middle age
that faults on the quake line
no longer hold, and the mind's endangered
thoughts are sanely closed.

He has fixed his star and bayonet
to the girdled sedge
of dimpled lawns, brought down the tine
of burdock and stickle,
the invisible wreckage of tender fires
floating in his head
like willet in the shallow rain barrow.

The agitation grows.
The youngest rifles out the kingfisher
        with shoulder butts
to the heart and spine. What is visible
        he thinks of the bird's
thrust back to his mind's midsection
        will be mourned by night and gone.

The Cholo has in mind the burlap flag
        in a Paris field
his father charged before the hollow
        cost of life was drawn.
For him the Sahara springs an ocean,
        the Pacific, barren
lots of sand. Killing the imaginary

        is an artist's craft
he sports with death for relaxation.
        He will not scare
into oblivion, nor a pique of mercy;
        he will not praise
the godless creatures of the world,
        the barrio, or *the man.*

The Willow Father

chopped down palm sunday on the yard laid holy
thursday punched across the neighbor's fence like Jesus,
        the neighbor's
tree we climbed for monkey balls and jumped
snapped like runner boards beneath by brother's bed
        bugs
hid the night the neighbor called us hunkies and the son's
a bitchin' willow father swore he'd eat his words or die
        writhing
sore there beneath the shed I hid my, oh my
cheeks red as dusk swollen by the sun during
        passion
friday never had so much hell-stone on the willow father's brow,
my brother Thomas said he hadn't heard the neighbor's word
        for days
across the yardway's fence I stared gravely doubting Thomas
sure the willow gone had disappeared into the neighbor's mouth
        with crab apples.

The Holy Ghost as Eighth Grader

At the Holy Trinity Prom where we were
boys, flattopped and heartless,
and dancing the slow dance
our black patent shoes imagined,
mirroring halfway up the tartan pleats
the soft girlskin of argyled knees
we liked to love the most,
Sister Eve in black lace shoes, dashing
round on roller skates
politely breathed, "Please leave,
leave room for the Holy Ghost."

And doves flew in where breasts intended
eyes and minds to gather, the floor
still reeling out of beat.
Guilt was meant for thieves, not boys
or girls half-crouched and dancing, legs
a full arm's measure apart, hearts
rubbing space like knees
with no conjugal consequence. We imagined

all the thrills reserved for gods,
how the Holy Ghost, confessing
old-age nuns with age-old sins,
found a cheap skin's thrill
beneath three layers of cotton briefs.
Every dance, slow or fast, that waltzing king
of nubile guilt we couldn't bear
was having more of God's given body
than we were. And wouldn't share.

The Tombs of Pechora

The Russian monk reminds us with our first step down,
that in procession each cavern is a burial of light.
Beneath our feet the cinder wax surrounds
the carvings of our passage into blindness. We create

our faith through loss of vision or in words we fail
each day to resurrect. In his litany of saints,
a thousand monks, box on box, tossed in shale
to shore a fortress, molder in their moats of silence.

In their caves beneath the sallows of St. Nicholas,
blindworms swell in rain to cross their borders;
a poet carrying lilies to Carmelius
hears the chanting in his candle's flare and flicker.

Each bulb of light beheaded pays for God's sedition.
Skulls, like crowns of state, pass blindly in succession.

Beckett Had Only One Student

As a tutor, Beckett taught only one
thought to a farmer who had pushed
a stone up pasture with a log,
            how to add
a syllable to the name of *God*
and reverse direction in the space of letters
from the dauphin *to* to the expanse of *ot*,
and to skip the space that followed
as a symbol of regret.
            And to wait
like Job before all meaning
doubled worry to a hundred *ot*.
How to push by only breathing,
            to and *ot*, *to* and *ot*.
Until his death the tutor
had only one thought to direct,
and the student one syllable to suspect.

VI / OCCLUSION
In the Age of Communication

Delivering Newspapers past the Cemetery Dead

The flames no longer steam
their private dark. Nor the streetlights
stoned by slingshots
marking distance we would run
before they cut us off. Save us, dear lord,
all paperboys from life deformed.

        Now the moon, night lizard,
that curls once about the stone,
hangs its traffic eye above a plastic rose
to blink our passing by. Watch us leap
the body mounds down Stonehead Road
to leave our words in paper bags
like flags on crocket thorns.

        Praised be the kobolds
who read obituaries as births.
I still see their eyes in manholes
and on the raven's daily cross
they hang lost souls like hoary lamps.
Let them wear the faces they repair,

the headline trolls,
stealing breath from swollen lungs
for arts and leisure at home.
Midnights in the vault's cold shale, lounging
where the talk wire runs to suburban beds,
the lost paperboy no one's found
is talking dirty to a beer bottle
disguised as a telephone.

He is taking calls
from neighbors missing newspapers.
He knows who's reading them and where.
Look beyond the hammock and the beveled rock.
A night light has just snapped on.
The dead have moved into our living rooms.
They read our comic strips for art
and make our televisions home.

Blueprints for a Mall

Where the library leans on columns now condemned
into a subtlety of parts, suffering itself, the whole
foundation chipped to cubes no higher than a ledge,

we are able now to brace the soil mix
with rods, tie the beams to heights of space
impossible to imagine. We have even learned

to still the rolling earth with slats of steel
and pools of ball bearings, lure the quake
into a fit of writhing. The gutted stacks within

like monoliths lasered by the sun
no longer ladder up to blinds beneath the ceiling.
Dust has fingered shelves with hieroglyphics,

and where the books are rooted the mind is no longer
bound to moorings of a former age. We will build
on the ruderal of the uniformly trivial.

Out of cubicles bare and mottled in the hobbied
hand of penned graffiti, we will expand
to stalls of commerce, gin and brandy,

and boast profusely on things profane.
What gains we make the wrecking ball will fathom
deep into the spills of our remains.

As for conscience, ban the librarians,
dead since Dewey. We've seen them old as ceremony
crack the spines of tissued books, incanting

codes in verse and gold Cyrillic.
Before all language paths the way to tyranny,
why not build additions to our suburbs

like syntax to the properties of words?
Why not read the blueprint of a mall
as fingers pointing infinitely in all directions

between what's gone and what's about? The future
is a spanner with jaws at both ends to lug a bolt
as if it were imagination we can do without.

Rilke on the Conveyor Belt
at Los Angeles International

A rick of pages, it falls hardly noticed
into motion, and down the track, unspined,
it cycles time between a rucksack and laundry.
A book no thicker than a wallet or a comb,
it is the unworthy carry-on, newly bought,

colliding with a carpetbag and steamer
on the unlikely navigation into being
where it's not. Each passenger has watched it
circle more than once, a bold intrusion
into the archipelago of things familiar.

There is no fixed point of concentration,
no laughter, no elation when the eyes dissect
the slow descent of baggage into orbit
as if in taking up an armstrap, each handler
slews a body to the spars of his shoulder.

Had Rilke himself fallen, unbound,
lying in united state, he would have passed
unnoticed by the baggage check or porter
who fail to think it odd or such a pity
to tag him at the lost and found.

How many miles had his words trespassed,
how many cities, alive, unread
among all ports of authority, a gold leaf
of art so grand in the pall of memory
it gives the mind encouragement to survive.

Unless unsung like a soldier's duffel, duty bound,
fear spreads its tarp along the spine of language.
Creation can end this way, abrupt and final,
like travel to the ends of the world
with no intent or vision but destination.

The Warehouse of Apostrophe S's

In Prague the apostrophe was in one day,
the next day out. With no genitive use for S
on signs along the river drive, they built a barn,

and trading alphabets, stitched new consonants
like threads through marocain or straw.
When no one asked where the S had gone,

a boy had thought to claim it thinking
his the lone possession of a single *mine*.
He asked, can nothing belong to someone

or to something other than no one? No,
the apostrophe, they said, had gone to hanging
in the cupboard as a hook for cups,

as a cradle for the moon, a crescent
or croissant, a sausage link or other such
oddities of curvature at brunch.

A Russian swore he used it as a sickle
for half a century, never thinking once
to flex the muscle of his arm.

A cat had spanned it boring as a yawn
or a lash of pointless exclamation
in the center of his eye. And now the vagrant

sees it lying round as parentheses
on nicks of furniture, in barley soups,
or loaves of bread he's picked in halves,

and sometimes as derision in a laugh,
but mostly on a question when like its meaning
possession has lost its basic point.

The Mayor Boils a Speck of Dust
FOR THE "YOU KNOW" GENERATION

One day we are walking in the desert,
the next, entrancing on a verb.
The mayor asks us for a speck of dust to boil.
The rain has moved to Eastern earth.
We had never missed the water,
reason being absent in the West.
North and South our hands had mimed a language
for the tongues we mottled in our mouths.
But while the words are thinner,
and sentences are worse;
the subjects, once agreeable,
now disagree on course. Syntax bows
to "you know," and simile to "like."
And while the mayor boils dust
to gain a speck of water,
we will talk, you know, into the desert
and verbalize, like, you know, our verse,
and dust will fill a fossil
for the law Pascal our mayor quotes,
that while the pressure in a fluid
spreads equidistant to every border,
dust will be rationed coast to coast.

We Stop the Universe with Study

Nothing, no one mourns
the loss of memory
when it suffers memory of loss.

It is enough to explain the absence
of black slate, the buried currant,
bluebells hitched to hayrakes,

why the stream no longer circles
hedge before the bottlebrush
consumes the spring angelica.

Fire has its own way
of behaving, objects to inhabit,
firmaments to create. Memory

is at a loss to defend what is not,
what denies transition in a thought,
or what changes forever

the behavior in nations,
why a border knows no limit
in the art of moving space.

We stop the universe with study.
Language turns to stutters. Memory
is one man's trap, silence is another's.

VII / SECLUSION
Premillennium

The Water Wheel

I saw in the turning of the great wheel
a millennium complete and stood in the dark
where on a slip of sand the poet dreamed
of a cradle no larger than a tomb, believing one,
whose time had come, might lead him out
of the bear's cave into the forest of suns.

I have run from what is never there,
from the atom's teat and the bomb's scare,
and the bomb's whore, devastation,
from all that whets the wind or like a vulture
feeds on air, from every cybernote
that rivers out with force and speed,

and have screamed at wood with all my might
that in the everywhere a god might hear
a wingless crow cry up that he be found,
a molting snake beg back his skin,
a desert rock sing out to tortured lips
that water sins in hiding underground.

I have studied blades on knives,
on grass, on tongues, in fires and anywhere
the ass has gone who carried Christ
to dish out crumbs, and foraged the gutted skull
in whose intestines, like a bone, thought
was swallowed whole and hollowed out,

and heard the terror, the reason's intercession
in each prayer, when, blindly, words would sleep,
soundless, in the cave of echoes, dreaming Esperanto,
and loathed to watch the sphinx and crow digest
each other's beliefs with mirrored pretension
that in wooing God, the mind is dead.

And now I see where sunlight sifts on wood so fine
the laths descend like spokes into the water's breast,
a child is crucified, hung beneath, near dead,
and breathing out a thin wind of motion, rises to condemn
the universe of civilizations, in each turn
returning him to breathe, to hope, to drown again.

The Board of Selectmen

At Walden Pond the woods have wished
to live deliberately; at least, till fall
the woodchuck's palate spares its buds,
and loons, downwind, have barely risen.
It's time, the Board has ruled,
to forge all paths away from nature's business,
reckless as a highway deer,
and done, we'll charge it interest.
Bind it to a levy, referendum,
give it teeth to grow in fear
like wolves from independence into freedom.
Pass new laws of leisure; the Board will vote
to select each perimeter of distance
the red-wing hawk may fly
or birch, in line, may bend in pleasure.
Roads will be paved, foundations laid
to give of each, a finch and applewood,
a viewing angle. Habitats will grow
like nuns into elegant neighbors.
Why not build our mansions
in the air? In the Middlesex County,
that's where they should be.
Now plant populations in them.

History

believes it has a memory,
the taut loom of past,
full of distance, time, and space
all of thought will gather.
It forgets to remember
the chestnut leaf in March
that wind keeps grieving
in the cornice of the Arch
or the dial of a linden's shade,
measuring the sun's walk across a wake,
or any point of light diminished;
the obelisk on Pont Royal,
whose lamp, a mist to the night bateau,
forgets to remember the barge Lutece,
lathered in a pug of rust,
its scull thin as a paper cup, drifting
past tobacco tills on Rue du Bac.
History wants to be a bottle
pitched from a primer's mouth,
the nipple, supple as the Invalide's dome,
the flow of future all eternal.

Only in the dim view of a tourist's eye
does it remember
to know all things in reverse,
how the camera shutters space
to lose all darkness,
how the hoar leaves frost
at the blossom of light
as if the past were only minutiae
for the time being. Nothing
enters history without memory
aging at its source.

Lines of Succession

They paint the hands as clasped together,
sisters, each a critic on the opposite
slate of an easel, the world split in two
by views of paper, the oldest searching
further than the white dove's leap
to where a bridge or tower rises
thick as boots out of mud, out of water.

The other, younger, watches chairs as dancing
down a stair and skillets circling,
round as faces, the beast of whom had better
tiptoe through the blue of clouds
or brown will paint it up-side-down
and bump it hurling into ground.

No matter what the day or sky, the brushes
slake along the torn stitches of the rain
to where the infant, in his gown, approaches,
first to paint his line of succession,
now to scold the world's order. Crisscrossing
strokes like an old dilemma, he reigns a tyrant
to their democracy. The bones of chaos now remain.

An Immigrant Playing Violin
in the Neighbor Wood

Father would not laugh with us publicly
when we walked the willow out of the house
to Levine's, the wood seller, to have
the branches pruned for studs and joists
and walls with skins, thicker than teak.

He would not laugh with us publicly
when we foraged the neighbor's home foundations
for splinters, sawdust, the white floss of laurel beams.
We straddled planks, naked, nosing sleep
in the fragrance of sapping oak.

Once in the ghetto's shadow of his private forest,
he shaped a violin from the heart of a river
and walked that perfect pine-wood proudly,
danced the rhythm through the rain
of its fine woman's body.

We would not laugh with him publicly
when the arm's string broke and something silent
in the gut of earth began leaving all the trees,
all the forests of his body. In the hills of America,
something freed in the house gave birth.

The Astonishment of Living

I saw beneath the spreading elm
two talking girls with rainbows
in their eyes. I saw their lives
on separate shores of the river
yield up their buckets to the falls.
Every drop was bathed in the fragrant
shawls of eglantine. Every leaf, in wind
rising up to comb each branch,
sent a whisper out along the banks—
let go. Lose all the breath in rain
and every strand of light in fog.
Let go of the tongue's crow
until it sings along with rocks
and runnels as if it were divine.
Let go of honored sky and earth.
Let go the horizon in between.
Lose all the sunlit undulations
of the season's wheat. And sing!
Call out to seeds, to grass, to all
that breathes into the pores of stones.
Let go the sovereign moons of space,
the celestial lulls of aureoles,
breathing out a planet,
pulsing out its days.

And where the stars ignite in showers,
let them fall. Recite the moment's song
that tomorrow wind will bring in squalls.
Free the century's melody as you would
a line or burden down a well.
Allow the astonishment of living
one reed or willow, feeding
swallows through a hungry night
until they weary of elation.
Let all buckets fill, all loss be light.
I saw two girls weaving rainbows in their eyes,
and daughtering in me their dreams, I grew
astonished by all conception,
the frail grandeur of life.